T0064305

Celebration of Self—

My Journey

Judy Gail Kirk

BALBOA
PRESS
A DIVISION OF HAY HOUSE

Author Credits:
Family, Kerese Thom, Natalie Hobbs, Kirsty Wright, Lynda Hood, Shenaz Cobb

Balboa Press books may be ordered through booksellers or by contacting:

Balboa Press
A Division of Hay House
1663 Liberty Drive
Bloomington, IN 47403
www.balboapress.com
1 (877) 407-4847

Because of the dynamic nature of the Internet, any web addresses or links contained in this book may have changed since publication and may no longer be valid. The views expressed in this work are solely those of the author and do not necessarily reflect the views of the publisher, and the publisher hereby disclaims any responsibility for them.

The author of this book does not dispense medical advice or prescribe the use of any technique as a form of treatment for physical, emotional, or medical problems without the advice of a physician, either directly or indirectly. The intent of the author is only to offer information of a general nature to help you in your quest for emotional and spiritual well-being. In the event you use any of the information in this book for yourself, which is your constitutional right, the author and the publisher assume no responsibility for your actions.

Any people depicted in stock imagery provided by Thinkstock are models, and such images are being used for illustrative purposes only. Certain stock imagery © Thinkstock.

Print information available on the last page.

ISBN: 978-1-5043-4193-6 (sc)
ISBN: 978-1-5043-4194-3 (e)

Balboa Press rev. date: 10/20/2015

Contents

Dedication

This wee book is dedicated to my Gran, who lovingly
showed me the Path and God who constantly
illuminates the way along it.

Acknowledgments

To my glorious family, animals,
and soul sisters: Kerese, Kirsty, Lynda, Natalie and Shenaz.

Thank you for unwavering support and love
Keep shining!

Celebration of Self

This book was originally written and self published in 2007 using pictures I would have loved to experience, I have gratefully been able to substitute everyone with a real image unknowingly until now, 2015!

The Wave

Harness the force
Light up the fire
You will be amazed at the source
Step out of the mire

Magic is the flow
Be careful not to gloat
For that unbelievable glow
Will set you afloat

Sing, dance and swim
That wave is deep within
Don't stick to its rim
Dive deep within!

JGK

Umhlanga holiday

Michael and the Labrador

1

Chapter One

Our childhood annual "get away" holidays were spent at the coast, mostly Umhlanga, together with "The Smiths", my folks' best friends. I clearly remember the times I spent on the beach collecting shells, swimming and building sandcastles. It was a time we had to all be together and see nature in Her glory.

My brother, one holiday, "adopted" a stray Labrador on the beach and so that holiday was especially fun with our new found wheaten friend. He would run up and down the beach chasing after us. I think my love for nature and Her creatures was reinforced on this vacation.

As the sea in all Her glory, provided an awesome retreat for the "Kirk and Smith" families, it too provided a sense of awe for me. Her energy was so constant, so powerful yet so unassuming, it was all consuming yet still within the crashing of Her waves. These immense powers led me on a quest to attempt to harness this energy and dive deep into Her waters.

I therefore took up scuba diving many years later, which is now an absolute passion of mine. My first diving experience was in Mozambique where we were blessed with amazing whale shark and dolphin sightings whilst on scuba. As my life has evolved through still and turbulent waters, it has been the power of something Greater, something all consuming that prompted me to write this book – this glorious force we have so freely available, yet so poorly utilized, loved and believed in – **ourselves**.

You see when I was a child I wanted to please the family, the pets, even the sea that I was good enough! I embarked on a wondrous journey of looking for external recognition to fulfill my internal void. I studied for sixteen years so I would be "someone". Don't get me wrong, I love what I do, but my reasons where purely to help others, inadvertently negating my own needs. Growing up in a family with a totally selfless mother, and trying to get the attention and love of a distant father reinforced my belief that self-care was "selfish".

I would often sit on the beach with a strong sense of "knowing" that one day I would make a difference, but not being aware that difference, would start first and foremost from within! I am only now aware of how intuitive I am, what a blessing!

My sweet souls; as you journey with me through this wee book called "**Celebration of Self**", you will notice that I have no recipes nor formulas – my objective is to create a spark, a slight stir and ultimately the awareness of how wonderfully glorious and special you are as you are!

I have been blessed with a wonderful quality of life; filled with wonder, joy and adventure. I have travelled extensively; experienced awesome moments of joy and sorrow; read amazing books and been mentored by wise, special souls whom I will share with you in "**My Journey**" the second part of this book.

Nature's rhythm

Quieten the mind
Soft and still
Pulses of sound vibrate all around
You are the legend
Never lose focus or get left behind
The flow is your friend
Nature is the soul
So rise up and get out of your hole!

JGK

2

Chapter Two

Love, like the sea, is such an amazingly powerful force. A feeling so intense yet so removed when we focus outside ourselves. When I lived amongst the turbulent waters of life (out of choice and lack of awareness), I battled so to comprehend this force; boy did I want this feeling to fill me, but the question was how, after spending so long yearning, chasing and "failing"? How was love the key when it caused so much pain? Thankfully, I read awesome books like "Women who love too much" by Robin Norwood and "Love is a choice" by Hemfelt-Minirth-Meier, which ignited a dim light deep within me, and thus I started searching...

Having being scientifically trained as a physiotherapist and medical doctor, energy "healing" was something I become aware of later on (second part of this book: **My Journey**).

Thanks to an awesome Reiki Master – Paddy, whom I went to visit whilst experiencing an unhappy life phase, taught me many wondrous things.

The most powerful awareness's being:

"Peace is surrender and acceptance"

"Know your value and make sure others do too!"

"Everything that happens is right!"

Around this time, another wonderful role model blessed my life – a very dear psychologist – Annette. Wise beyond her years she helped me overcome my absolute fear of divorce, you see I was never getting divorced as I had come from divorced parents, I knew better! Yip, so much so that I sold my soul for a while, but gratefully regained it on my return home to South Africa.

The third glorious professional role model who believes in my gifts both medically, personally and intuitively is – Patricia – a psychologist and the mother of an ex-boyfriend. She would listen excitedly to my visions of a Holistic Medical Centre treating people as "whole". She is a great listener and I thank her for inspiring me to dream of S4S Consultancy, Sunshine for the Soul, and the need to love and be loved! Patricia has subsequently moved to live in the United States of America with a true soul companion she met at 60 years of age. What a blessing!

Sunshine for the Soul is composed of five branches- S4S Eco Zones, Shift, Community Upliftment,Training and Products. The primary vision of S4S (Sunshine for the Soul) is about connecting people and projects, empowerment and upliftment of individuals and communities everywhere, for total well-being. S4S is wellness leading to joy! Sunshine for the Soul is a global organization that assists people to rediscover their inner joy.

Please refer to my website for further information:
www.s4sconsultancy.co.za
or watch out for my next book titled :Sunshine for the Soul"

I realised that wanting all the love in the world and receiving it all, would never fill my inner void. It was such a powerful day at a friend's game farm, when whilst reading and quietly appreciating nature, this glorious book "Authentic Self" by Sarah Ban Breathnach hit a chord deep within. The 360 degree turn from outward to inward began and what a rotation!

I know we have been blessed with amazing gifts and talents that will only ever reach full potential when we believe and celebrate **ourselves**. Self-love is one of the hardest acts I am practicing, I believe it does not become automatic overnight nor in a week, I believe it may take me a lot longer.

I love birthdays and Christmas, anything that involves surprises and celebrations. A very special soul played Seal's song, "Love Divine", to me at one of my special birthday celebrations. I am not sure if he was aware of how profoundly that struck and reinforced the spark within me, that we need love; **self-love**.

I now realise that my passion for the sea was a metaphor for the love I so wanted. The energy is constant, has ups and downs but never fails to continue to exert its affect. I had dived deep into the sea and looked in all its nooks and crannies for sea life but never realised how this life force runs deep within me...

What a blessing to give up the "control" and surrender to the all-consuming power, more knowledgeable and knowing – **love.**

I wish, that as you journey along life's highway you receive an abundance of love; this magical potion, and may your tank never run dry...

Love Divine

It's tough I know
Don't go with someone else's flow
Cos their love will never make you whole
Dive deep into your soul
Love, love and love your sweet self
Cos then boy does the flow go
Yip all over the show!!
Thank you for the awareness
Light, love and solid harness

JGK

3

Chapter Three

My fascination with the sea has been strongly coupled with a humbling reverence I have for sunshine, and the amazing energy that the sun provides... hence my emblem for S4S Consultancy, Sunshine for the Soul being:

Sunshine has an amazingly positive effect on my being, especially my energy levels. This became ever so apparent when I lived in various dark and cold Northern hemisphere countries; no amount of positive thinking increased my ever-diminishing energy levels!

I was unaware how this very energy; like waves and love, needed to be let into my soul for self-nurturing. We are then able to radiate all this glorious energy outwards but only once we are internally on fire!

Have you ever experienced that awesome light at sunrise in the bush, or a beautiful sunset touching your inner being? Harness that moment my friend, live within those seconds and light up your being with its power.

Yes I know sometimes we get gripped by total darkness, other times dull patches, it is in times like these we must keep the waves and love deep inside of us alive. We need to believe in our Divine, unique, awesome, God-like selves as self doubt is so consuming and energy wasting.

In these dark phases we need to just "be", detach and choose to use the moments we are experiencing, as an opportunity to become aware. Sometimes these unconscious, recurrent choices result in repetitive behaviours which are not in the best interests of our self care; we may have lost temporary sight of our path or we may just be needing a space to connect again - **mind, body and spirit.**

Sunlight

Rays are the fruit of the soul
Sweet, sensuous and solid
Love all creatures even the mole
He makes holes
Yip to allow the Light to shine
Deep within his home
It's so fine
Light comes and goes!!

JGK

4

Chapter Four

It is so fantastic that when we allow the waves of love to flow deeply within our being, our Light is so bright that inner peace is the outcome! All these magical ingredients are being provided for by an immense Higher Power- God / Buddha / Spiritual teacher – it's your journey, your associations.

This elusive and so distant peace; something that resonates deep within us once we have chosen to be blessed by God's grace and felt the beauty of this. We have our own way of unlocking this tremendous power and the reality is you alone hold your key. I beseech you to take the step, believe in your unending beauty within and open the lock; life will never be the same again!

Peace is self-awareness of all our self-sabotaging, self-loathing and self-defiance, erased to leave behind a slate so pure and innocent. Are you willing to take the leap and live?

Peace is to hear another but not to speak; it is to "see" into their lives but to know that it is not our job to "fix" them but to rather honour our own journey and vision. Peace is stillness, focusing beyond the *monkey mind,* one of my endless challenges.

Peace is all knowing, yet standing still, for you are here, I believe, to **celebrate self**, before moving into another's terrain.

Peace

Piled up, lists to tick
Give them all a flick
Sit quiet and still
Life's one big treadmill
If that's your choice
No need to make a noise
Carry on running bud
'Cos I'm off and still!

JGK.

5

Chapter Five

I have been blessed with unbelievably loving grandparents, mother, brother and sister. We have travelled many roads, together and alone, I am eternally grateful for "having chosen" them as my family links here on Earth. I am grateful to my father for having met my mother, as their union produced me!

The power of combined love, I believe, can never be overestimated for which I am grateful. It was by harnessing this and turning it inward that I was honoured to become aware of how amazing our souls are.

I so believe that if we, as humans, honoured and took responsibility for the state of our lives, collectively, we would cause a loving revolution!

As stated by the Dalai Lama

May I become at all times, both now and forever

A protector for those without protection

A guide for those who have lost their way

A ship for those with oceans to cross

The power

Have you wondered about atoms?
Yip weird, if you think
So don't, lift the stink
Laugh, live and simplify
Power of stillness
Lies in those atoms very vibration
No need for hills to equal stillness
It's that power deep within that regulates all!!!

JGK.

6

Chapter Six

So, as we reflect on our lives thus far, what a joy it is to see how things have happened because that's how it was meant to be and how powerful we are to manifest what we want...

My question to you today is, "are you afraid of your Divine greatness, your unique power of self?" If so, be gentle with yourself, slowly combat those fears knowing that we write the script for our lives and surely *only the best is good enough*!

The end - the beginning!

And at the end,
Send heavenward
The burning arrows
Of your perfect faith

- The RuneCards, Rune 15,
Teiwaz, The Warrior

My Journey...

As you journey towards Celebration of Self, once realised, may you feel the true joy of selflessness – the need for no self!

7

Chapter Seven

What a privilege it is to be called into the "healing" profession. The beauty is there are so many avenues, specialisations and fields of interest. I began my medical training in a truly traditional mould, as a physiotherapist through the University of Witwatersrand. It was a well-structured course with small groups within which we were taught physical presentations of overuse injuries, infections, sports injuries, neurological trauma etc.

We were taught how to "fix" the physical form with many options at hand, examples such as laser, ultrasound and massage. We formed wonderful friendships and shared many fun times together. The lecturers were generally very helpful and friendly, which made time learning much more bearable especially around stressful examination periods.

The pressure of a group of high achievers was palpable especially at these times. We were so young and serious! Freedom is attained with a deliberate choice, that choice (voluntary or involuntary, conscious or unconscious) is not one I realised at this point, as I knew knowledge was power and that meant head down and study! We were fortunate enough to have been exposed to a broad spectrum of physiotherapy and so many of the students began formulating their ideas into specific directions of interest. We had to participate in rotations through the various hospitals / clinics which was an eye opener to the "real world".

An experience, which remains highlighted in my mind, was the time I spent at the cerebral palsy unit at Chris Hani Baragwanth Hospital. I was struck by how awesome the staff was and the beautiful souls of the children in the rehabilitation process. Although their physical limitations were markedly noticeable, their eyes danced full of light and love. I became aware that there is a bigger plan for us whilst in this Earthly existence. Another soul stopping moment of mine was related to a little boy named Elvis, who had been abandoned in one of the paediatric ward cots, he was awaiting adoption. He was one of the most beautiful bundles of joy I had been blessed to share time with. I would visit this toddler and play with him; he was so bubbly and precious, and hence I nearly adopted him, the reality being that it was not to be.

The opposite spectrum of living is that of death, the introduction to our cadaver was an unbelievable surreal moment. We named her "Margee" and we gratefully respected the fact that we had been given this body to learn and visualise our human anatomy. Certain things never leave you: one being the memories of these moments and secondly, the smell of formalin for a solid year! We were blessed with knowledgeable "table doctors" who helped us make the dissection process more humane.

We were exposed to so much knowledge in such intense phases that my head felt like it was going to explode! I developed headaches unbeknown to me at the time, a manifestation of my emotional stress of achievement. I had eye tests, blood tests and eventually a CT scan where I was told I have a hole in my brain!!! Fancy that, not a beautiful thought, when I chatted with the neurologist, he said it was of no significance and thus no cause was found. Later I was to learn how incredibly sensitive I am to energy especially the people around me. I was living in my unconscious realm of work; play (very little) and the chosen mentality that life was "hard". I did really well in all my exams / tests whereby my headaches would subside and my self-esteem would increase.

I felt limited with the physiotherapy research aspect i.e. a lot was based on "touch and feel good" but how does one quantify this and prove it? I was blessed to be awarded a scholarship for all my studies, so combined with my great grades, I applied to med school whereby medicine became my next avenue of training. During my physiotherapy days, it started becoming more and more apparent how "abnormal" I felt relative to the crowd.

I started having amazing intuitive feelings about what was "wrong" with patients – now that is not acceptable in the book of conventional medicine! I remember an exam patient; anonymous it was supposed to be! I walked in and said it is your heart hey? She nearly did have a heart attack and so, my "strangeness" grew until I decided it was enough and stopped listening. I used to go with my beloved Gran to Sunday church services and there I felt I was able to be more open and fly (so to speak) with my feelings and expression through song. Here I felt God's Spirit move me and I was able to get many answers to my questions through song lines.

Only now do I have the awareness of how beautifully I was being guided. I still felt limited by certain "box" beliefs and I wondered why, if all religions want love and insurmountable joy, we feel there is a right and wrong way? I started questioning choices I was making and started experiencing and reading about other faiths / beliefs / religions – what an amazing time (it still is!).

Physiotherapy days ended with my degree and new hardship of larger classes, greater perceived pressure and "doctor-hood!"

8

Chapter Eight

I joined the third year medical class and once again it was new beginnings, whilst my physiotherapy friends stepped out into the "working" world. I did to some degree, no pun intended, envy them as I needed a source of income, so I started my own little practice from home, rendering physiotherapy treatments (afterhours), whilst running the local hospital's physiotherapy department as well.

I was not sure how I did all of this whilst studying full time, today I am aware it was / is – "Divine Grace"! I enjoyed the working experience whilst studying, which seemed to balance things a bit, certainly more than the physiotherapy days, which I found more intense (smaller groups and loads of work!).

My love for spinning classes started during this time, I used to pop out to the gym down the road in our lunch break. I am now aware that this was my meditative de-stress time (still is!) I found that if I missed out on this sacred time; my body and especially my mind, knew all about it.

It is interesting that my mind often does not recall many details from the past, yet what I do remember is very vivid and intensive. For example, I have no recollection of dates, times or events of many things from the past, yet I remember the day I wrote my boyfriend's car off outside a police station! I was so cheeky that I refused hospital treatment and my poor Mom had to fetch me. I remember even more clearly his Dad sitting opposite me the next day outraged with what I had done, hence my boyfriend became an ex and I felt a right twit!

This is where my interesting experience, or should I say mystery, with alcohol started. My parents got divorced for many reasons, the most prevalent one being my Dad was an alcoholic, bless him, he subsequently died of liver failure. I was unsure whether my alcohol intolerance was related to a psychological fear due to my past, or a reality, nevertheless I ignored the signs and attempted to outwit my body. I was unlucky at this game because the fitter I became the less I was able to drink (naturally!) yet the worse the side effects became i.e. it felt like a bus had run over me in the morning. Yes I know that is how it feels as a lot of people would tell me... but my bus was not one it was twenty!

My answers came at a much later phase, as you will discover as we travel through this part of the book "**My Journey**", the transformation of traditional to holistic or if you like unaware to aware or even unconscious to conscious state of living.

Medical studies I felt were very theoretical, preparing one for medical illnesses (e.g. diabetes) with the focus on disease not the individual. Thus at times I found myself talking about the "pancreas" instead of the person with the "pancreatic problem". I guess one way of coping is to label things, so we are able to focus on the disease and curative medicine negating the impact of that disease on the patient. This also excludes how the patient may have manifested her / his disease through dis-ease!

I was blessed to have worked with highly intellectual people whose focus was on curative medicine and doing it well! Failure, or lack of cure, was not an option and if so, it was rarely spoken about. This is why when later in my life; I came across the beautiful fields of care called Mind Body Medicine, Palliative Medicine and Holistic Health, they resonated so strongly with me. Sure I had read about them extensively whilst studying but I had not experienced them first hand so to speak!

I got the tap on my head on our graduation day and thereafter we were cloaked and pronounced doctors! My second degree was now added to my list of achievements.

Boy was my self worth "styling" yet still lower than the high I had initially imagined. Initiation by hell fire was the next year – internship – not only was it physically and mentally exhausting but I also sustained a needle stick injury. The patient subsequently died of AIDS and I had to tell my fiancé that I might become HIV positive. I had to start ARV's (anti-retroviral drugs), which thankfully prevented this.

What a learning curve, one I pray I have learnt so as not to be repeated! After the craziness of internship it was time to fly out into the big wide world. I forgot to mention not only did I have a ruptured appendix a few weeks before my wedding that particular year, but I was also hospitalized for a Quinsy abscess! Was my body trying to connect and get my attention or what?! I found it really difficult saying "no" and expressing my truth – hence the abscess of the tonsil! My interpretation being throat chakra obstruction, how amazing we are!

I continued to walk a very "hard" path full of struggle and turmoil, how unaware I was that I was about to enter very dark nights of the soul for a prolonged period. We decided to do the "travel" thing before we "settled down", so off we went to the UK where I worked in a crazy post, four days on call and four days off.

It had sounded glorious; I had even planned on travelling during the four days off! I was so unaware of the intensity and volume of work in those four days on call that I ended up sleeping for the four days off! If the locals don't do the job go figure! My partner battled to find work in London so his self-esteem dived whilst my energy levels did too! It was a nightmare created all by me! (Us).

He ended up getting an awesome job in the Channel Islands, so off we went to Guernsey. What I experienced there was so intense and so extreme on a soul level that I ended up in a major depression as I continued to ignore my inner voice and **true self**. Instead of making the most of the moment I fought and I fought. I hated everything about the choices I had made and literally died inside. I will never forget the joy I used to feel arriving at Jan Smuts / OR Tambo airport – HOME. The peace was so indescribable as my soul started to dance during those rare times.

This depressive episode was very frightening for me, as I had not experienced it first hand, whilst having observed others suffering from depression, made it very real for me. The reality set in, whilst I had to choose to listen to my inner voice and take responsibility for my current state. I stumbled across a book called The Zen Path through Depression (P. Martin), which was healing honey balm for my lost soul.

My partner was beautifully supportive, yet I was in no state to receive or give love as I had no sense of self being ego ruled. Once my journey started, honouring my needs, I knew he would not return home with me, so I went back to the island and confronted him and we parted ways. I was no longer able to ignore my true soul's yearnings. He subsequently married a Guernsey girl and has two children, I am so very happy for him.

During those years abroad, I did have many joyous, light, travel moments. I experienced many beautiful moments with people suffering from similar circumstances; the more I travelled, the clearer my inner voice became and my intuition heightened. I feel that once I had worked through this phase of the dark nights of the soul, I surrendered part control and started "seeing" why I had gone through the pain and illusion of dissolving my ego and embracing my path of knowing and "healing"! I not only met beautiful souls, I was exposed to fascinating ways of holistic care. I worked in teams with various healthcare professionals and therapists, I learnt the skills of acupuncture and other alternative / complementary medical treatments, which was very empowering.

I feel this is when the beauty of all traditionally based medicine merged with higher notion of care – leading to spiritual awareness within me.

9

Chapter Nine

I felt slightly bewildered...what was I – physiotherapist, doctor, spiritual practitioner?

This is when the voice inside me started shouting *"it is not what you are, but how you facilitate awareness."*

I listened for a brief period, whilst meeting an awesome woman who introduced me to energy "work", facilitating awareness. This prompted me to do a Reiki course and then once again my intuition started awaking from within. I listened to parts of my calling and started "seeing" that through the eyes of one's soul there are no coincidences, only miracles. I still struggled with inner turmoil, life is "hard" and what is fun about all of it?

I worked in various fields, from Hospice to HIV care, whereby I was prompted to study further in Palliative Care, it being the "closest" specialty to my love- Mind Body Medicine. I studied long distance, through UCT (University of Cape Town), where I completed my third degree, a Masters qualification, over a period of two years and loved doing the research thesis (much to my horror).

The beautiful members of Palliative care team, which I headed up at Johannesburg General Hospital, together with myself, conducted the research for my thesis, which focused on quality of life, on a group of hospital patients. It addressed all aspects of holistic care (i.e. spiritual, emotional, social and functional). The results were astounding, how the effect of a "minute" intervention by the team (e.g. disability grant), had on elevating our patients' quality of life! These findings were a great motivation for further interventions.

My initial introduction by the staff at the hospital was "here is the Doc who holds patients hands whilst they die." I knew there was far more to this than meets the eye, or should I say the "soul". The publishing of the fact-finding "Quality of Life" research in a local, prestigious journal helped the scientific minds understand slightly more about the role of Holistic Health (that being person centered care as a "whole" being with all the facets met, that being spiritual, emotional, social and physical). I now had a dilemma of integration of my traditional medicine, energy awareness and knowing...

I was drawn to working outside of traditional medicine boundaries (i.e. hospitals, practices) and started working from a wellness house whilst running the HIV clinic in the local tertiary hospital. My awareness of synchronicity started to blossom and I feel this opening spiraled my awareness of the mind-body connection. I started having more and more intuitive "knowing" of what the patient's illness might be before they spoke and started receiving "messages" for my clients.

This really terrified me; gratefully like-minded therapists who taught me so much about trusting "my gut" and learning to "let go" surrounded me! I experienced many beautiful "healing" modalities, which I never knew existed, what a blessing they were and still are. These not only accelerated my own awareness but also greatly assisted clients who resonated with different forms of therapy- hence the team approach.

I now found myself on a rapid journey towards awareness of **self (Celebration of Self)**! My ego then started to feel unsettled, as my meditation and meetings allowed my awareness to note the illusions presented by ego and the various unclaimed parts of myself. How was I to "wish" for a soulful, loving relationship based on unconditional love, when I did not unconditionally love and accept myself?

My ego continued to feel threatened, the more I became aware of my intuition, the more the fear rose within me. I eventually stopped listening and that is when my first near death experience happened.

I was due to meet up with my Mom at a private game lodge in Botswana for a wonderful holiday she had received from work. I was driving alone and at the best of times I find it difficult to stay grounded, so whilst I was floating in my world, I suddenly became aware that I was lost. I had no idea where I was, I saw a sand road coming up and a voice said, "Do not go that way". What did I do? I continued driving and took the route along the sand road, the next moment I lost control of the car and thought, "this is it"!

I let the steering wheel go whilst my life flashed before my eyes like an old-fashioned movie clip. In slow motion I saw the grass on the one side of the road, then the other side, as we zigzagged out of control. I thought that this is just how my patients had described it and braced myself for the inevitable; the car was going to roll. It was so peaceful and surreal, I was no longer afraid.

I felt a powerful force and big "angelic" hands took the steering wheel and the car came to rest on the opposite side of the road. I was still mesmerized when the adrenalin and tears set in, I looked at my car to see if I had just had a wild dream or a hallucination, there were the pieces of grass stuck in the bonnet and scratches along the side of car doors.

I had survived a near death experience and why? I now know that Spirit wanted me to listen to and trust my intuition. My life slowed down for a while whilst I noticed an amazing thing- my judgments of people disappeared and so did the "hard" Judy. I started becoming aware of warm, pink, fuzzy, loving feelings and was drawn to pinks, previously the colour being very much loving orange! The colour pink is often associated with unconditional love whilst orange with creativity and sacral energy.

I had been wearing the "mask" of a serious, hard and logical gal and suddenly when I was no longer giving advice nor judging, boy did relationships and roles rapidly change! I stopped being "the social organizer" and suddenly people started disappearing from my life!

I noted an amazing awareness of self-focus and a beautiful feeling of radiant love possessed me. I continued in my role as a "healer" but now with greater awareness of mirrors; both of my patients and personal relationships being reflected back at me. I began embracing my "defective" pieces through these reflections, instead of reacting with judgments out of my contracted consciousness of "old" I became detached, yet responsive.

I have been blessed to have met many awesome souls and only now do timing and synchronicities make sense! Behind all this turmoil and pain I believed I needed in order to live, I "saw" Universal suffering and craving for Wholeness; full of peace.

I have subsequently been "diagnosed" with a sulphur allergy, hence my intolerance of alcohol, previously mentioned. I honestly feel it was Spirit's way of increasing my receptivity, prior to which, I had unconsciously detoxed and stopped caffeine, some other amazing steps Spirit initiated to increase my awareness. My life progressed along with greater issues of self-doubt, self-esteem and searching which heightened as 2007 began.

10

Chapter Ten

I began integrating all the beautiful things I had experienced and learnt along my life's path thus far, both the reasons for the pain and pleasure, started becoming clearer. My meditation and yoga practice increased, yet my periods of peace were transient, I was still searching for love externally in the "perfect" relationship; feeling unfulfilled, as I did not have the traditional life of family, kids and the white picket fence, which I misguidedly thought I needed, to be happy.

I have been blessed with absolute abundance, life long, so it was not poverty consciousness but more feelings of emotional isolation motivated by ego. As my self-doubt increased, my separation from the perceived intimacy within my relationship became apparent.

One day, I experienced an event that affected my life forever, a close friend of my brother's died tragically in a car accident and on my way to the funeral she "came to me". I had just finished a spinning class and I was feeling great as I drove "alone" to the funeral.

The cold presence engulfed me and her voice said, "Jude, I need you to tell my boyfriend and my Mom especially, that I love them and they must find peace." I was "frozen" inside, she then said "I know you don't believe me but I have come to you as you are "open" and so to validate my authenticity, I will switch the lights on and off a few times, on the right hand side of the church. I am also aware of skeptics and narrow minded people around, nevertheless I know my boyfriend will be receptive to you if you first mention my favourite shirt and give him this message of love".

Well, I tell you, I have goose bumps as I write this, I am only able to vaguely remember the overwhelming intensity I felt. Now I was confronted with my very "self" that I had been running from, the still-knowing, intuitive one. The feelings of absolute judgment by others and the medical diagnosis of "psychotic" came to mind!

If I was to voice this, I risked losing all my protected, hidden "self", I had shut out with my degrees and other wonderful aspects, to expose the true me- God focused light worker. I sat through the service filled with trepidation and sure enough the lights went on and off, I did as I was asked to- I spoke to the particular people and felt the judgments of people flow my way. Amazingly for the first time I had verbalized my "craziness" and did not fear it! Thank you Spirit!

I chose not to channel dead people, as I do not feel comfortable with it, however I promised to embrace my intuition completely. My ego clearly did not think this was a good idea, so I continued to deny my true "self " and function out of ego. My fears would come and go, as I attempted to go back to my "safe" ways, ignoring Spirit.

On the 19th February 2007 I took ill (my grandfathers 87th birthday), two days later I was in hospital, in the Intensive Care Unit (ICU), with bilateral pneumonia – medically unexplainable, as I was healthy, well and fit three days ago. Thanks to Spirit, wham bam, along came my second near death experience in three months. The angels were around me again (my precious companions) and my life flashed before me. This time I did not feel peaceful, I felt afraid. My Gran said to me, "Jude get on with it, you are blessed, embrace it." She died many years ago but is very much one of my spirit guides and wise voices I am blessed to be guided by.

So here is a traditionally trained doctor with a broader knowledge of illness, "dying" in ICU. I then had very low blood pressure due to septicaemia and experienced awful physical pain due to repeated injections and treatments in all forms. I made a choice to get out of the dark nights of this soul journey as soon as possible as I did not want to repeat the lengthy overseas experience (**Celebration of Self**).

I recovered rapidly yet my energy levels lagged, I experienced unconditional love from my friends, family and partner which all made sense! I had a beautiful "healer" visit me and he said, "things will never be the same", I did not relate to this until a week later when I experienced this unbelievable peace. This peace was larger than life and no matter how full of turmoil things were around me I felt peaceful. I realised I had been forced to "let go" in a big way – all illusions; self created sabotage and my past and current relationships.

I still ponder over how amazingly radical the change was and yet how fabulously freeing it has been. Thanks to this second near death experience I now embrace Spirit and "listen" to my intuition. I am so very grateful to have seen past my ego and I am now attempting to embrace my true "self". I don't feel mentally deranged nor strange rather peacefully stable, living in this Earthly reality day by day.

Peace reigns and I am free to create awareness and facilitate this awesome Universe to its rightful state of bliss and collective consciousness of Oneness.

I was performing an energy treatment on a beautiful soul, she sat up at the end and said, "Did you get sick on the 19th February 2007 and you are unsure how?" She said 2007 is the year when self-doubt issues intensify (fancy that). On the 19th of February the portal over Johannesburg was opened – as channeled by Michelle for Master Kuthumi – so here was my spiritual answer.

Thank you for the final confirmatory "understanding" which occurred at a beautiful Oneness evening (Deeksha prayer). The speaker was amazing, explaining that no matter how hard one tries to meditate and obtain enlightment and universal peace, one rarely attains a permanent state. Through grace and biological repatterning this peaceful state becomes constant.

A gentleman in the audience asked about the stages the speaker had discussed; those of initially feeling unconditional love, then joy, then total peace and awareness of collective consciousness, he then asked, "Is it possible for this to happen after serious illness?", "Sure" was the reply!

Here was yet another confirmation of my true path and my journey of awakening. Together with the intellectual awareness and the comprehension of truth, an astounding joyfulness followed, as all the misperceptions of normal self-consciousness are lifted. If people see that the nature of the Universe is love, and that we are all part of an undying conscious life force, it is very difficult to experience fear or doubt. I am ever grateful for the awareness, love and light and guidance by God.

In the book "50 Spiritual classics", it is discussed how cosmic consciousness, in turn, causes an intense awakening in some humans. Bucke describes it as an acute awareness of the true "life and order of the universe" in which a person experiences oneness with God or universal energy.

Characteristics of illumination

Bucke came up with a list of historical figures, which in his view had clearly achieved cosmic consciousness: Jesus, Buddha, Mohammed, St. Paul, Francis Bacon, Jacob Boehme, John Yepes (John of the Cross) etc. His list of "lesser lights" included Moses, Socrates etc.

Bucke's discussions of these cases make for fascinating reading and form the body of the book, Cosmic Consciousness.

He noted the following characteristics of people who had achieved cosmic consciousness:

- Average age at illumination was 35
- History of earnest spiritual seeking e.g. love of the scriptures or meditation
- Good physical health
- Enjoyment of solitude (many on list never married)
- Generally well liked or loved
- Little interest in money

The features or indicators of cosmic consciousness include:

- initially seeing an extremely bright light
- appreciation of separateness as an illusion i.e. everything in the universe is one

- appreciation of eternal life as a fact
- after illumination, subjects exist in permanent happiness. They actually look different, and have a joyous expression
- no sense of death, fear, or sin- Whitman, for instance, moved among dangerous people in New York but no one ever harmed him
- those who have experienced illumination recognize others who have, yet find it difficult to express what they have seen

Bucke made some other interesting points:

- most experiences of cosmic consciousness happen in spring or summer
- the level of education is not a factor- some of the illuminati were highly educated, others had little schooling
- illumined people generally had parents of opposing temperaments e.g. a sanguine mother, a melancholy father

My wise yoga teacher once asked during a beautiful class, "At what point did we become human doers and not just human beings, learning to be? the faster the pace, the faster the doing!"

So as oceans and butterflies have ups and downs, rising and falling, so too must we attempt to be aware of our ever-changing landscape, honouring change whilst continually reshifting our centre, our balance back to the moment, the only guarantee we have, the present moment.

I am grateful to have been inspired to write my book out in nature whilst being privileged to watch animals and birds teaching me about being! Thank you Divine Spirit for allowing me the power of words to reach the souls of many who read this. So be it!

I now surrender I / ego to the bountiful beauty and peace of this life, effortlessly experiencing the moments.

Thank you and may peace become yours.

Butterflies

Thought of in many cultures as soul birds
– symbols of the spiritual life – after death.

"Had I known the glory
of my future's boundless flight
I would never have feared the darkness of the
short cocooned night"

Author unknown

Dr Judy Kirk is a qualified physiotherapist and medical doctor, and has a Masters degree with a 20 year career focus on wellness and holistic health. Throughout Judy's extensive medical career, her awareness and understanding of the powerful mind-body connection - not only in day to day living, but in healthcare as well - lead to her seeking a way to fulfill this need in society...

So when Judy completed her Masters degree qualification in Palliative Medicine, she became even more inspired to drive a campaign for empowering people to live a life of joy, and thus was the birth of S4S Consultancy - Sunshine for the Soul - by God's grace. Let's face it, we all need Sunshine for the Soul!

It is clear that we need to give as much attention to the quality of our lives as we do to what we accomplish and produce. Well-being, health and peace demand a change in attitude and approach to many activities we engage in through our days (Deepak Chopra). Life is a gift – a twilight state of dreaming.

Reducing stress and fostering calmness rely not just on the art of detachment, but equally, on learning to be more aware and sensitive at times when we are likely to become lost in mental activities; in busyness or preoccupation. This is when we build up stress and sacrifice mindfulness and connectedness. The beginning of anxiety is the end of faith, and the beginning of true faith is the end of anxiety.

Love - "total acceptance without judging"; remembering to have fun and to laugh often!

Keep shining xx